GRANDMA MARGIE'S TALES OF ELIJAH AND ELISHA

Written By Dr. K.T. Zulkowski

Published by Mz. Kim Productions
4263 Tierra Rejada Rd #151
Moorpark, CA 93021
www.mzkimproductions.com

ISBN: 978-1-962106-22-1

Printed in United States of America
First Printing: November 2023
Date of Copyright: July 5,2023

For permissions, please contact: Mz. Kim Productions
4263 Tierra Rejada Rd #151
Moorpark, CA 93021
www.mzkimproductions.com
mzkimproductions@gmail.com

Dedication

To my dearest friend and sister in Christ, Diane, I dedicate this book, "Grandma Margie's Tales of Elijah and Elisha," to you. Your unwavering faith and friendship have been a source of strength and inspiration in my life. Just as Elijah and Elisha shared a deep bond and journeyed together in their faith, I am grateful for the journey we have embarked upon as friends in Christ. Your presence in my life is a reminder of God's love and the power of Christian friendships. This dedication is a testament to the emotional connection we share, Diane, and the profound impact our friendship has had on my life. May these stories of Elijah and Elisha touch your heart and serve as a reminder of the extraordinary things that can happen when we trust in God's plan. Together, let us continue to carry on the legacy of faith, love, and friendship. I also dedicate this book to my late grandmother, Margie, whose legacy I carry on. Grandma Margie, you were a woman of faith and wisdom, and your love for storytelling ignited a passion within me. As I share these tales of Elijah and Elisha, I am reminded of the stories you used to tell me, weaving lessons of faith, courage, and miracles. Your memory lives on in my heart, and it is an honor to dedicate this book to you.

With heartfelt love and gratitude,

Dr. K.T. Zulkowski

Educational Value

"Grandma Margie's Tales of Elijah and Elisha" offers several educational benefits for young readers. Firstly, it introduces children to important biblical figures and stories, fostering their understanding of religious texts and traditions. The story also highlights the significance of faith, trust, and obedience to God's calling. Through the examples of Elijah and Elisha, children learn about the power of prayer, the importance of helping others, and the impact of God's miracles in people's lives. Additionally, the story encourages children to develop a personal relationship with God and to seek His guidance in their own lives. Overall, this tale promotes moral values, empathy, and a sense of wonder, while nurturing spiritual growth and understanding.

Grandma Margie: "Once upon a time, in a land filled with miracles and prophets, there lived two extraordinary men named Elijah and Elisha."

Zipporah: "Grandma Margie were they like superheroes?"

Grandma Margie: "In a way, my dear. They were chosen by God and performed amazing miracles."

Zion: "Wow, Grandma Margie! Look at Elijah! He's surrounded by fire and wind!"

Grandma Margie: "Yes, Zion. Elijah had a special connection with God, and He showed His power through him."

Zipporah: "Why did Elisha leave his plow, Grandma?"

Grandma Margie: "Elisha knew that following Elijah and serving God was more important than anything else. He left everything behind to become Elijah's faithful disciple."

Zion: "Grandma, what does the Bible say about Elijah and Elisha?"

Grandma Margie: "In the book of 2 Kings, chapter 2, verse 9, it says, 'Let there be a double portion of your spirit on me.' Elisha longed for a double portion of Elijah's spirit."

Zipporah: "Grandma, how did they cross the river?"

Grandma Margie: "With God's power, Elijah struck the water with his cloak, and the river parted! They walked on dry ground."

Zion: "Grandma, where did Elijah go?"

Grandma Margie: "In 2 Kings, chapter 2, verse 11, it says, 'Suddenly, a chariot of fire appeared, and Elijah was taken up into the heavens.' He was taken by God in a miraculous way."

Zipporah: "What did Elisha do after Elijah was gone, Grandma?"

Grandma Margie: "Elisha picked up Elijah's cloak, a symbol of their shared journey. He knew he had a great responsibility."

Zion: "Why is Elisha tearing his clothes, Grandma?"

Grandma Margie: "Tearing his clothes was a sign of mourning, but it was also a way for Elisha to show his determination to carry on Elijah's work."

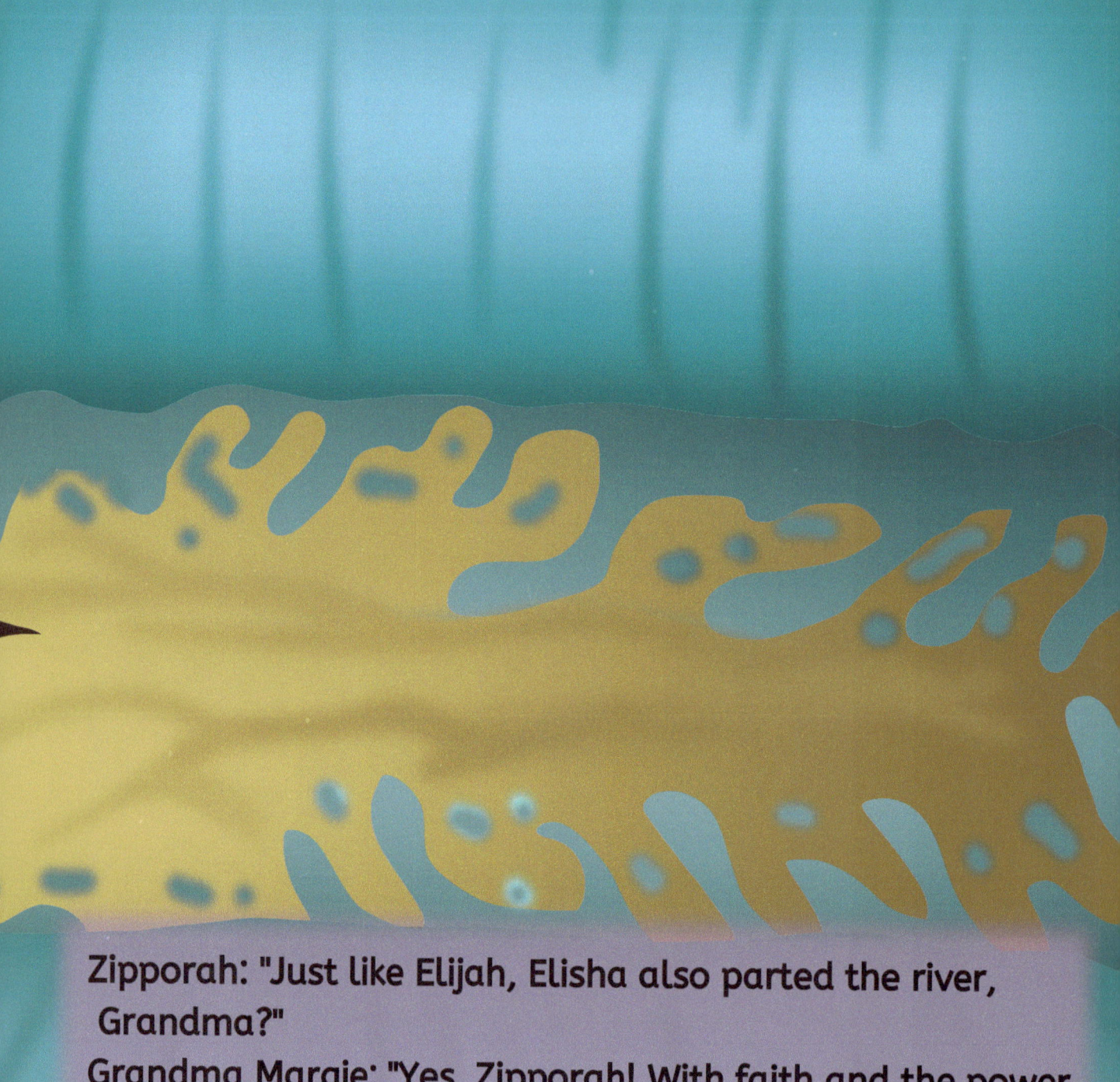

Zipporah: "Just like Elijah, Elisha also parted the river, Grandma?"

Grandma Margie: "Yes, Zipporah! With faith and the power of God, Elisha struck the water with Elijah's cloak, and the river parted again!"

Zion: "Grandma, what miracles did Elisha do?"

Grandma Margie: "In 2 Kings, chapter 4, verse 42, it says, 'Elisha performed a miracle, multiplying a small amount of food to feed a hundred people.' God's power was with him!"

Zipporah: "Did Elisha heal people too, Grandma?"

Grandma Margie: "In 2 Kings, chapter 4, verse 35, it says, 'Elisha prayed, and the child's life was restored.' God worked miracles through Elisha!"

Zion: "Grandma, did Elisha help people who were sad?"

Grandma Margie: "In 2 Kings, chapter 4, verse 7, it says, 'Elisha helped a widow by multiplying her oil, so she could pay her debts.' God's provision was abundant!"

Zipporah: "Grandma, who were those people with Elisha?"

Grandma Margie: "In 2 Kings, chapter 6, verse 17, it says, 'Elisha prayed, and his servant's eyes were opened to see the angelic army surrounding them.' God's protection was with Elisha!"

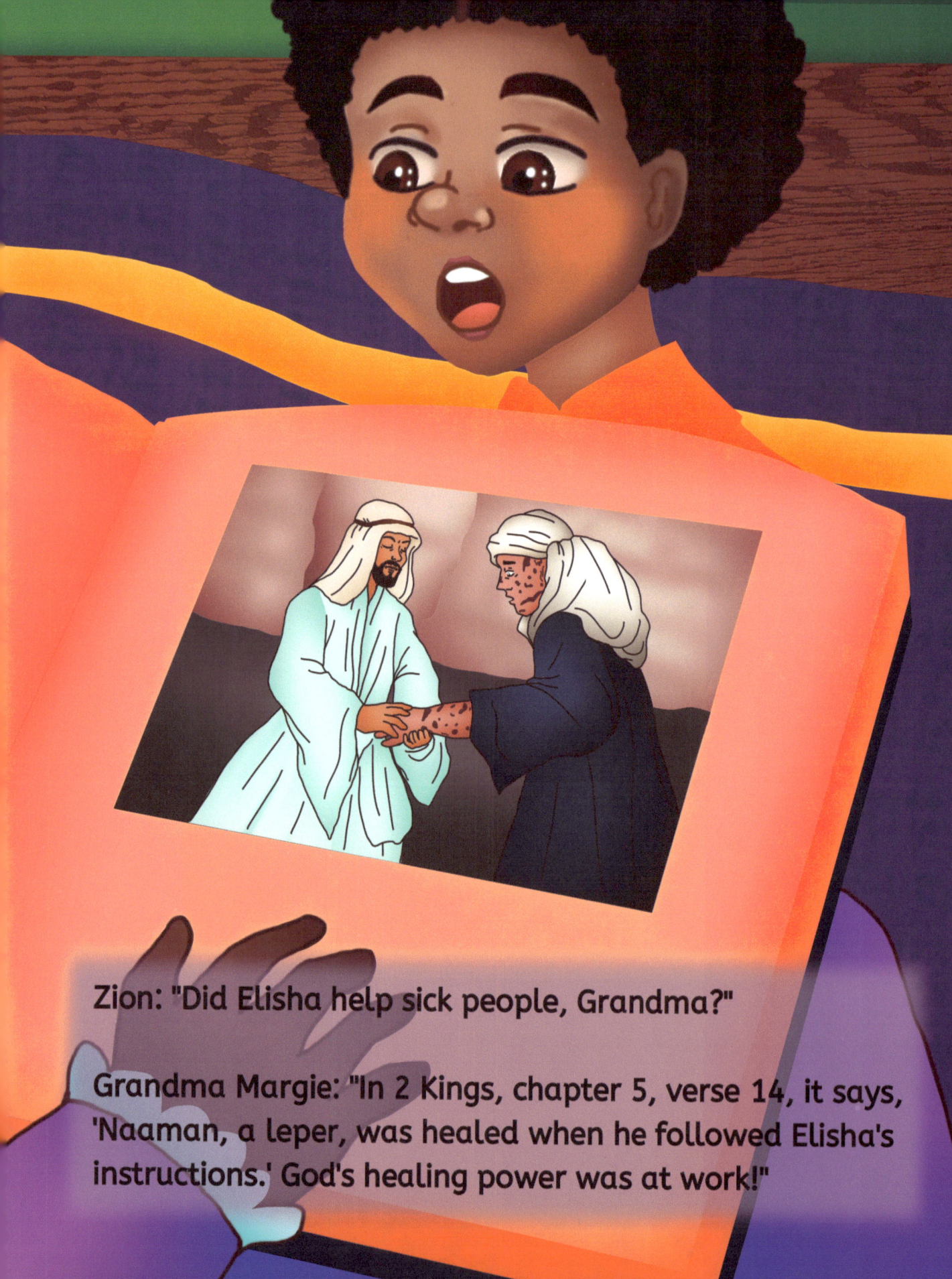

Zion: "Did Elisha help sick people, Grandma?"

Grandma Margie: "In 2 Kings, chapter 5, verse 14, it says, 'Naaman, a leper, was healed when he followed Elisha's instructions.' God's healing power was at work!"

Zipporah: "Grandma, did Elisha bring someone back to life?"

Grandma Margie: "In 2 Kings, chapter 4, verse 32, it says, 'Elisha breathed into a young boy's mouth, and he came back to life.' God's miracles were extraordinary!"

Zion: "What happened to Elisha, Grandma?"

Grandma Margie: "In 2 Kings, chapter 13, verse 20, it says, 'Even after Elisha's death, a dead man came back to life when his body touched Elisha's bones.' God's power continued to work through Elisha!"

Zipporah: "Grandma, these stories are amazing! Elijah and Elisha were so close to God!"

Grandma Margie: "Yes, my dear Zipporah. They trusted in God and performed incredible miracles. We can learn so much from their faith."

Zion: "Grandma, can we also have a close relationship with God like Elijah and Elisha?"

Grandma Margie: "Oh yes sweet Zion! Just like Elijah and Elisha, we can have a personal relationship with God through prayer, reading His Word, and trusting in His guidance."

Zipporah: "Grandma, can we also help others and perform miracles like Elijah and Elisha?"

Grandma Margie: "Indeed, Zipporah! We may not perform the same miracles, but we can show God's love by helping those in need, being kind, and spreading joy wherever we go."

Zion: "Thank you, Grandma, for sharing these incredible stories with us. We feel inspired!"

Grandma Margie: "You're welcome, my dear ones. Remember, God's power and love are always with us. Let's keep our hearts open to His miracles and share His goodness with the world."

Grandma Margie: "And so, my precious ones, the tales of Elijah and Elisha remind us of God's faithfulness and the extraordinary things He can do through His chosen ones. May His blessings be upon you always."

The end

Author's Note

Dear Reader,

Thank you for choosing to embark on this literary journey with "Grandma Margie's Tales of Elijah and Elisha." As the author of this book, I am thrilled to share these captivating stories with you.

The inspiration for this book came from my own experiences of listening to my grandmother's enchanting tales during my childhood. Just like Grandma Margie, my grandmother had a gift for storytelling that transported me to different worlds and taught me valuable lessons along the way. It is my hope that through this book, I can pass on that same sense of wonder and wisdom to you.

The stories of Elijah and Elisha are not only fascinating but also hold profound lessons that are relevant to our lives today. These biblical figures faced challenges, triumphs, and moments of doubt, just like we do. Through their stories, we can learn about faith, perseverance, compassion, and the power of miracles.

While this book is rooted in biblical narratives, it is also a celebration of the bond between generations. The relationship between Grandma Margie and her grandchildren, Zipporah and Zion, is a testament to the love and wisdom that can be passed down through family connections. It is my hope that this book will inspire readers to cherish and learn from their own family stories and traditions.

I encourage you to immerse yourself in the world of "Grandma Margie's Tales of Elijah and Elisha" and let your imagination soar. Whether you are reading this book alone or sharing it with loved ones, I hope it sparks meaningful conversations and moments of reflection.

Thank you for joining me on this journey. May these tales bring you joy, inspiration, and a deeper understanding of the timeless lessons found within the stories of Elijah and Elisha.

Warmest regards,

Dr. K.T. Zulkowski

Abrazo.